AF413697

Bengt O Björklund – Days of Dark Thunder

i

DAYS OF DARK THUNDER
BENGT O BJÖRKLUND

Foreword

I first met Bengt through the National Beat Poetry
Foundation, at one of their annual Festivals.
Imagine myself, Paul Richmond, Carlo Parcelli,
and Bengt sitting around discussing art, poetry, and
life.

It was a good day and is a fine memory.

Bengt impressed me with his openness and his
intellect. I enjoyed his readings of his works, and I
solicited him almost right away to write a book for
my fledgling publishing house…which he got
around to, eventually. I am glad he did, for his
words are almost like magical incantations, like
prophecies, he is a true Amomancer, a true
Qoheleth, and the world is better for him being in it
and sharing his soul with us.

Enjoy!

William F. DeVault
New Generation Beat Poet Laureate
US National Beat Poet Laureate Emeritus
The Romantic Poet of the Internet

Dedicated to my dear wife Gertrude Nilsson Björklund.
Imagine that! Almost 30 years have gone since we first met.
And we have two beautiful children to prove the love we
have.

To William F. DeVault and his team for turning my words
into a beautiful book.

To Deborah Tosun Kilday for keeping the fire of the New
Beat Generation roaring.

To all poets, artists, musicians, actors, jugglers, workers and
bums I've met in my life.

To life itself.

ISBN: 979-8-9995232-2-8

where can I the jingle jangle
    of days
in constant disarray
    find a light switch
for the cold piers of old Stockholm

I nod to the dark water song
as if to mend a long past
    cajoled
into keeping perch and pike
        dancing dancing
in dark water brooding

warlords have guns for breakfast
    they return
with whispers of ire from battle
    the old and the dying
are all in bed

full of songs
    that smell of salt
        lost
    among the crackling wires
where blue flames
        burst
    into the empty upper floors
        I sing of a dark transgender Jesus
of fish and wine

war finds me lost
        in disarray
     riding hot canon images
aimed at death's
        dominion rolling
            cemeteries in fashion
into foul water sermons
        where vile men
            will not dance
nor seep through the kitchen floor

Bengt O Björklund – Days of Dark Thunder

she was stuck
  in a tin foil fantasy
    avoiding spiders
any kind of spider
  selling comics
    at the atomic market

she ran with old rainbows
  selling her unique style
    to any bystander
when winter came
  she'd hibernate in cyberspace
    calling all boys to the bonfire

telltale whispers
      crawling
through days
    in bondage
blue skies
   will not
      subvert
         cruel meanings
   of hate's intent
billow in
         poplar trees
the distant war is a threat
   wherever
     you
        are

      there's ire
   in the autumn
         wind
      the dying
   of the day
begins
   at dawn
cheerful executioners
hoist flags
     of bright
        extinction
the very air we breathe
     burning
all of it
     burning
     burning

small people
    die
in small drawers
  small people
making a racket
    in case
they're allowed
    a second chance
with their small boots
        blazing
in small dreams
  of
     grave
        solitude
and a sullen
  blush
  of
  shame

vagrants fill
    the
    empty
    spaces
small people
leave   behind
making
        small
              fires
              in
        the silence

their weather
  is always
    in a good mood
  and the grinding
of small mountains
      sigh cheerfully
  in small return

Bengt O Björklund – Days of Dark Thunder

sudden shifts in observation
    finds an old man
among sparrows
      in hasty flight
from naked cemetery bushes

a keeper of lost parks
    he walks
      with gravestones
aiming for bright new visions
    and more silence

his pale thoughts
     lift
  daring the chilly day
    to feed his eyes
he rests his case on an old bench
    feeding the wind his
      presence

alone at daybreak
    he recollects
     days of childhood
a cold rain
       falling
feeds a grey resignation

he remembers the schoolyard
    where life was cheap balm
     and the market
       full of little merchants
    selling it all
  for a run in the woods

Bengt O Björklund – Days of Dark Thunder

I see signs in the sky
worried faces rolling
    running for office
in countries where flags
    burst into fire
    on any given day
ruled by the unfair and the dead

unselected and unruled
those with scars and tissue
    crawl in the solitude of I
for the sake of no war
    no killing
    no hate
they also reject indifference

steeped in still back water
weary men run for cover
    as tactile bombs
fall from the skinny enemy skies
    where dark rabbits
    do worry
about the end of time

streamed and crying
I see your need to grasp
    and understand
the dervish madness
    the spinning image
    of a life
as an oyster in a watery dream

Bengt O Björklund – Days of Dark Thunder

I see the dull I see
shaved Buddhist calamity on fire
    with nothing to say
breathing heavily
    in white man's
    privilege
bowing just for the sake of it

time is a walk to the cinema
before the posters are printed
    a dive into a blue pool
before the homeless
    leave their poor mark
    on the newborn baby
in a park at midnight

sometimes between here
and logs not yet ignited
    I dream of soya cream
whipped into labor days gone
    I will not yield
    or pray
this is but another day

pious men's relief
in dark slaughterhouses
    run red with religion
make animals bleed
    for the sake
    of being more than one
peddling dead fruit

Bengt O Björklund – Days of Dark Thunder

ruled by the fire of night
        stored in the afterbirth of all
    that descends
    into a here
where no solitude
            can relive the testimonies
    of silent extinction

dead men sell dead flowers
at the market where men
    go to war
            with nothing but pathology
dressed up for surgery

    so that night I met
your mother all done up
        in scorched finery
with a disposition for scorn

solemnity and weather
    ran for a seat
in the local portrait
            of Dorian Gray
various factions of stuntmen
    found their addresses
            sold to the highest bidder

Bengt O Björklund – Days of Dark Thunder

relentless in motion
    dire in intent
self-appointed lawmen
rule the after hours
with whips and threats
    of forgotten exposures

billboards praise you
whisper of a dying planet
    warn you
    of those
with rules for safeguarding wealth

you do not count them
    anymore
but even ants and slugs
must have a vote
    a say so
at the end of all goodbyes

Bengt O Björklund – Days of Dark Thunder

a sudden ominous hush
   finds you where
      shadows long
            for ordinary dying
or faint promises
      of something
            laid out on tables
brimming with old eyes
   where we all
   can dream in silence

give me your old mothers
   your children
      and
            the hole
   you left behind
  the two-time deceiver
      you once called a friend
         give me
your rapid violence
      in days
            when boredom
   stares at you from a kettle
      that will not boil

   burn me a bible
abort me a fetus just in spite
            drive nails into the flesh
of any animal of your choice
      kill
      any mammal
just for fun
            dump your toxic waste
in any live river or lake

       take greed
   to your bosom
        feed it
with your darkness

we are the last
   of the last
   holding on
      to a dying world
              with our bare words
      and all
      we can possess
        with a sense
      of a fading
      human dignity
we are the pale vestige
of an intention
        meant for
so much more
        than extinction
war and hunger

Bengt O Björklund – Days of Dark Thunder

go no further
  whip no day into night
    without shoes
      or the decency
    to keep religion
  under the Persian rug
            it took a thousand knots
      to feed a family
      for a week
        or maybe
just the weekend

guns meet
  guns depart
    mothers and wives mourn
  on both sides
      of the muddy trenches
  dug because
    one man wanted it all
      setting old restraints
        on fire

Wish me a cow
  or a horse
    a few chickens
      a turtle a few birds
        the sky is so different here
      where no muzzle fire
  ignites the summer darkness
        falling
        falling
          falling

there are birds
   lodged in our memories
     making noise
   as we meet the day
  wings that beat
   against our inner straw
lining the aging
   and the flight of days
burning like forest fires

at times we
   like sparrows chirping
      chirp
        chirp
in the bushes outside the church
   take our small hearts
    of longing and loss
     to funerals
      and chimes

birds will fly
   birds will sing
     no tears will fall
      from their beady eyes
  but we will cry
     when we hear
gentle doves
    in marble days
blending with sand
   and rolling water

Bengt O Björklund – Days of Dark Thunder

time to fetter the phantoms
  and feed the dead
to nail their dead pulse
    to the floor
where no wind will dance
      in silence
where I will creak
  and break
    and sing
to the ghosts
      that lived too late

I see shadows on the move
setting sail
  turning
    dying
into the art
    of blasphemy

curb the mad king
  dead to the sea
    rein his sick froth
      and his tales of sorrow
    burning like birds
  lizards or fish
hold his pompous thrust
  that only blank men
    can hear
      and heed

Bengt O Björklund – Days of Dark Thunder

so many shadows
    in my eye
where all rugged care
    rests
like quail eggs
        before hatching
    to the sound
        of waves rolling

I am a misfit
    in a world
        full of hate
    and greed

    I am a lonely man
crying in halls
    of no return
bleeding with booze
    and painkillers
        running naked
            in desperation
    drowning suffocating
        I will end

Bengt O Björklund – Days of Dark Thunder

it was the first day
    of September
the sea salt salesman
    lingered
in a grey afternoon
    with his torn pockets
full of gulls
    and terns
        screaming
at the surf
    rolling
        heralding
            the storm

who will be the bait
  today
    the sacrificial worm
impaled in silence

morning tolled
  with squid and bells
melted into the resounding ore

there is history
            in the old rock
where paleontologists
    still can hear
snails and ammonite sing
    in school stairways
        slowly erased
    by clouds
        of small feet

Bengt O Björklund – Days of Dark Thunder

this
October
I will not submit
to the voice I am not
meandering
through these woods
of yesterday
I am no more the puppet
you once knew
struggling
with
my strings

leaves
in dark water
smell
of dying
fills the barrel
with goodbye and ale
I will not hesitate
nor bargain
when crystal water
beneath the moon
breaks another
dark tale
to
come

I am the crow
you once
met
in the history of the flood
returning
over the scarred shore

the silence
singing
in your blood
where I will be
no
more

the All's
eponymous universe
never eclipsed
nor encircled
by time
or any other
scant human notion
of
incongruous perception
moves
in its own
fashion
with atomic leaps
and dark matter lullabies
galaxies
and star clusters
ejects
quantum colored light
long gone
echoes
of spectacular events
billions and billions
of years
ago

Bengt O Björklund – Days of Dark Thunder

there's a faint scent
        of dying
hovering above
        poor man's cradle
            rocking
            creaking
over dry straw fulfillment

stars of bleak anonymity
    continuously collide
        with foreign men
gathering in shabby stables
            somewhere
        in the Middle East

the land belongs to no one
        it's just land
        with no specific purpose
bound repeatedly
        to the next day
where man and beast
        constantly meet
in an all-embracive
        dance
an epiphany
        of lost grace
a longing amongst
        matter itself
a whisper
        a melody
hung from sky to cloud

serendipity ran
   down thirsty hills
before the dying
     of the I
beckoned in halls
       of no nurture
it fell into dreams
     of no more
standing on its naked feet
Sunday steeple mass
        haunts you
   pointing
        to the empty sky
weary men
       will weep and sigh
there will be
       no substitution

who will fly
       in the songs
of our children
   when we are no more
who will stir
       in dark days
   when brittle bones
        turns to dust
when promises answer
   a last call
from the final darkness

Bengt O Björklund – Days of Dark Thunder

we are all in a dungeon
    of poor vision
where pale images
        haunt us
            fading
into the original sludge
            that begat us
    in times long lost
in the great balloon
            we call the universe

it's all a bloody mess
        traveling
    faster than light
            just to make a point
  we will never understand
    the details
        we call infinity

burning freezing
    exploding
in a slow motion
        show
            I look for telescopes
        and
all saved receipts

do not worry little cloud
    full of hands
        chiming
    at late night
be sure to fold
    your memories
like winds on the run
        there will be
    a final reckoning
in time for bed roll

I saw dead men
    riding dead hardons
all the way
    to the bickering bank
sisters begging
        for more light
where the two-faced
        dare
balmy air tubs to run
for a different
        beach front

Bengt O Björklund – Days of Dark Thunder

money never fails
        to burn
ceremonious tables
     at nightfall
run a duck
     entertains the darkness
the striped
        and the old ones
with no certain marrow
can hear the jackdaw
        in the morning
singing the coming into void

remembering
  old sails
windmills on the run
    icy mornings
      bright sunshine
on my way to the silent crowd
looking for small bills
       fleeing
like scared pigeons
    at a harbor mass
I suddenly see
     the gap of time
grinning like a winding tale
  in a broken
    music box

Bengt O Björklund – Days of Dark Thunder

someone rinses your yesterdays
    in ice cold water
from afar you see hands
    firmly knead and rinse
all your mistakes
    until they finally
    worse for wear
regain their everydayness

small thoughts
    crawl like mice
in the old clock
    that stopped
    a long time ago
there is a faint rustle
    as small paws
eagerly move
    through the silent clockwork
you imbue the day
    with a kind
    of final farewell

all that lives dream
    animals
everything organic
    but tell me
does a stone dream
    lava
    that that runs
    beneath us
the air we breathe
    the water
    the wind
    the fire

Bengt O Björklund – Days of Dark Thunder

the earth that patiently
        waits for us

I hear dogs' whimper
    in dog dreams
it feels safe somehow
            the cloudy night
        sees me
as a fly on the wall
    anything organic
                is a witness
to the going on
        in our lives

Bengt O Björklund – Days of Dark Thunder

we meet sometimes
  where I go
    and you like I
look for a reason not to run
    with eggshells
      and pliers
        for a global office
no one has heard of

standard distance rule
  the birth of waves
      and ships
moored at midnight
    chiming
where are the promised seabirds
          welcoming us
  to the honey wine land
        where sybarites sing
and costly ceremonies
                    hum

steeped in vodka and history
   worn like an old tale
     running down
          main street
I do remember
         casual meetings
   at the Russian embassy
       drinking
with the minister of war

my old friend was pushed
    I'm told
in front of an Underground train
   at Victoria station
while pirates of the cocaine trade
invaded airports
    across Europe
there were strollers on the run

after a slow taste of the caviar
   there was a piano player
  dressed in b minor
     doing justice to Rachmaninov
       but we thought
       of Charlie Chaplin
    when the lights went out

Bengt O Björklund – Days of Dark Thunder

once the tide was blue sky
    a tram ride in the sun
a few words to make sure
    history moved ahead

standing in straight lines
    small men
    watch the grinder
turning all before them to pulp
    the sky is still blue

moonlit nights when lakes
    tend to look the other way
reed conspiracies sing
    in new and unexplored keys

the streets are swept
    by a hundred small winds
    and eyes on the run
weather is just another word
    for getting ready

suddenly is a condition
        past thin hands
                time chiming
            well
                is a stoic expression
interrupted only by
                dire
                solemnity
                and psalms
sung by the lost
                in empty halls
                of no insurrection
wired to fit the continuity
        when I and pale accordance
            fall short at midnight

never more you said
                raven
                being a sure bet
running for office
            in times of such cruelty
        and
        pale holidays
        filing for divorce
see me here and see me not
                we will always
                find a way to mourn
when repetitious days lash out
        finding us in bed
        with calling storms
        of history

Bengt O Björklund – Days of Dark Thunder

ravenous and dying
      on the run
terrestrial ailments
      flail
      and whisper
dry wood entertainment
     crackles in fires
     by the dark sea
surrender is no option
when weary men
      fall in silence
calamity
will rip their hearts apart
      serendipity
      will not sunder
   to any future
   in this
   say so here
where I is a kind of
you on the run

breaking darkness
            into
      more than one
                  takes but
                        a spoonful
            of wasted hopes
      and a pinch of sea-salt

digging deep
            into the pockets
            of dark days
      gone
      I find
my memories
on washing lines
      swinging
      in an April breeze
there's a murmur
at the back

the ore
      that sings
      in bells
where believers
have turned
      into sad fires
chimes for the not yet dead
      and the oblivious

Bengt O Björklund – Days of Dark Thunder

this is the night
    of Sirens
    cyclops
    and she
with snakes for hair
    this is a banshee night
where rumors
will find their wind

    days of pain
    and sorrow
will find a way to drift
    into numb waters
      guilt and shame
      will be a carpenter
running late for reckoning

Bengt O Björklund – Days of Dark Thunder

slow sleep
        haunts me in the dark
                futility runs along
                        just for the ride
                in our dreams
        we die happily
or screaming
        at the top of our lungs

Bengt O Björklund – Days of Dark Thunder

death at birth
    with your first breath

death by murky water
    and you are lost

death rolling in the surf
    smiling as you die

death walking with you
    every day and every night

death in the morning
    and when you fall asleep

death on your mind
    when everything looks so real

death is a shadow
    you cannot ignore

death is your name
    at the final door

Bengt O Björklund – Days of Dark Thunder

there are sparrows
              in my pocket
I keep them there
        to be safe
from ignorance
           and bad weather

I tend to peel
          my oranges upwind
just to make sure
        their fragrance
fill the wake
behind me

Bengt O Björklund – Days of Dark Thunder

mostly by myself
        I drive
hot nails
        and surrogate mothers
into a different kind
        of despair
every morning
    I tend to
sleep in
        due to bad weather
foraging
        in lost drawers
where once
        shiny cutlery
made statements
        of a world
dying
    to be done with

repetitious understanding
        will haunt you
        as day
turn into goodbye
        an old man once said
    when confronted
        with winds
that he had no objection
        being born as he was
into this world's sweet misery
        with one eye clapping

Bengt O Björklund – Days of Dark Thunder

there are birds of bad weather
                chirping in the afterbirth
                        wings of wild confusion
            soaring through the night
                    I will be the dragon eye
                            daring air to follow me
                                    in days of dark thunder

Bengt O Björklund – Days of Dark Thunder

crossing water
>> melting ire
>> morning salutations
early winds in trees

sublet dreams in cities
>> stop at roadblocks
> tend to bleed

where battleships roll
>> waves sing
>> seagull seaweed songs

men at war
> wake up at dawn
>> preparing for battle

blind cruelty roar
>> in days
>>> of distant thunder

a morning wind finds you
> daring mortality
>> with your own blood

Bengt O Björklund – Days of Dark Thunder

dining with the lost
                    I sometimes find a way
            to disembark
        without leaving my home

it's such a strange
        and uplifting experience
                to dance with
        your own vocabulary

there's a bumblebee
        spreading visions
                of a different world
                    where collapse
                        is not impending

so I tell my children
                tears are important
                    so is the wind
                        blowing in the garden

wheel me an ocean
        and I'll sing you a sky
                spell me a coming
        and I'll be there

Bengt O Björklund – Days of Dark Thunder

the night was a pale mistress
        whispering
                dark streets to life
                        invitingly
                                standing in doorways
        turning cars into songs
                coming from the jukebox

there is no place like here
                        where trams need no tracks
                where kites with wishbone tails
                        see birds feed their
                nestlings
                in days patiently in flight

winners at the lottery melt
        squalor into tin soldiers
                marching across the carpet
        parental anguish is a ship
                herding young islands

timed into a slow train
        on faded tracks of old
                turning history into
                        mirrors
        I remember landscapes
                fueled by transistor radios
                        and the raw crackling beginning
of rock and roll
        working class songs
                of love and putting food
                        on the kitchen table

seeded danced and happily tiled
        into a suburban
                happy-go-lucky
                        I can hear a saxophone
        and a dissed steel guitar
                rummaging
                        through my flower beds
        an Afro American voice
                demanding
                        see through cotton for all
        the sound of a Guitarrón
                dancing with the family bones
                and a bottle
                        of southern rum

Bengt O Björklund – Days of Dark Thunder

there's a red bus full of refugees
                at the busy intersection
            where celebrities will die
        for a fast selfie with the major
                tossing his hat to the wind
                    a red bus named war
                        tempts traffic
                            with electric
                    silence

                making new friends with soldiers
            stepping out of old newspapers
                the refugees sing
                    of arming their days
                        with blue cheese
                and old rifles
            streets will feed on them
                dancing into the end
                    fire will be all

Bengt O Björklund – Days of Dark Thunder

broken I
    walk
        sunshine
          to the final door
    I drink
        cool morning air
in a chalice out of control
        I leap to my feet
          and go for walks
            where for centuries
       many have waited for a path
          packed with particles
            of light

I fumble
    and call for winds
        to correct
          my mind's impediment

I have no shoes
        no money
    I am a lover
        of glass
    a javelin at best
        in days of thunder
dreaming of shortcuts
          and lizards
    wearing dogs and cats
        around my fake coroner's heart
          I do on occasions dance
        with the backbone of bright resistance
          fashioning faces out of clouds

Bengt O Björklund – Days of Dark Thunder

I am the opaque heart
    you once
    abandoned in snow
the here you relinquished
    for a bubble
    of invisible joy
a walk on the beach
    a dive
    into a different tomorrow

spring lullabies echo softly
    under the evening sun
        I'm still the antithesis of war
    the coagulating sound
        of wounds in fear
I am the death of a cricket

seldom in want of dreams
    I
    and all other I's
        rumble
    like dark thunder
        in days of no surrender
    there will be
        no tomorrow

    if the sky doesn't say so

Bengt O Björklund – Days of Dark Thunder

the wild side of Brazil
once folded hot suns
into a love dance
turned days into more cachaça
ice cold beer and kites hovering
high above the cliffs of Santa Teresa

the old tram fought its way
up steep streets turning
until the final stop
where the sprawling favela
rolled teeming alleys
down the precipitous side

Bengt O Björklund – Days of Dark Thunder

sleepy summer walks me
>a rag doll
>>in the soft breeze
to the teeming word market
>where all critics
>>tend to gather at noon
just to make sure the heat
>they need to suffer
>>will be in their final review

there's a creek you cannot cross
>if you are penniless
>>and lost
in the shadow of a giant chestnut tree
>a scrutinizer waits for you
>>but he will not punch your ticket
'less you can run him a bath
>without moving
>>or bring color to his pale cheeks

stories made of sand and water
>come and go with the tide
>>words on fire turn to ashes
unread books pave the path
>before he that can't see
>>the bare footprints
return in the afternoon

Bengt O Björklund – Days of Dark Thunder

intent is just another reason
to embellish all that may be of value
on any given market day

old language leans against
the slow burning
evening
collective reading was abandoned
already in the mid seventies
the soul was perceived
as electricity
it went rampant the next year
reaping the harvest moon

drool thee that do not feel free
when blackberry bells toll
for no reason at all
there will be
no
survivors

will I not be more
will days not say more
than lavender in a short flight
above my garden
with luminous ground
to feed

Bengt O Björklund – Days of Dark Thunder

telling tales of distant bells
                       bronze giants
         of yester times
                       I hear myself listening

I am today's undertaker
               selling obituaries to the bereft
        coffins come coffins go
            belfry bells will ring

Bengt O Björklund – Days of Dark Thunder

there's a moon on the run
        from bright war and indiscretion
            nights of dubious intent
                rule in favor of the stray one

vascular dreams will vessel flow
        only because they are fluid
            there's an inherit attraction
                that can turn any sea into a dream

find me a carpet to fly
        in days of raw solicitation
            find me a stigma to nourish
                when days turn oblique

during the performative years
        the coroner made a bold stand
            defending the flat ones
                and the very thin

rushed to hospital through traffic
        the old man could hear the dead
            speak of deeds and plain time
                laughing in the early morning

Bengt O Björklund – Days of Dark Thunder

cry not little girl
        in days of small thunder
    the ripping is of no consequence
          when the moon is on the rise
horizon is just another word
    for staying in bed

beasts and wild fungi dance
        in halls of yet to come
    there is no benediction here
          where the sky is a fool's curtain
chained to the roaring sea
    see the chimney sweep smile

pull up your socks and say
        with a gargoyled pose
    I will not pay for the porcelain
          smashed at serendipity's wake
do look out for dead people
    they tend to hang around

days of small thunder I give you
        and shifting clouds in a pool of hope
    the remarkable is the little bird
          you feed with your presence
as you wake up in the morning
    and go upstairs

Bengt O Björklund – Days of Dark Thunder

someone rinses your yesterdays
in ice cold water
from afar you see how the hands
firmly knead and rinse
all your mistakes
until they finally
a bit worse for wear
regain their everydayness

small thoughts crawl like mice
in the old clock
that stopped a long time ago
there is a faint rustle
as small paws move
through the silent clockwork
you imbue the day
with a kind of final farewell

all those live dreams
animals and everything organic
but tell me, does a stone too dream
the lava that pulses beneath the surface
the air we breathe
the water the wind the fire
the earth that patiently
waits for us

Bengt O Björklund – Days of Dark Thunder

I hear the dogs whimper
in their dog dreams
it feels safe somehow
the cloudy day sees me
as a fly on the wall
or an organic witness
to what is going on
in an incredible multistory

at times visions
images
and metaphors
will dance
in your head
yet you have
no words
that will turn
them into
poetry

Bengt O Björklund – Days of Dark Thunder

mostly by myself I drive
                        nails and surrogate mothers
          into a different kind of despair
              every morning I tend to
sleep in due to bad weather
                    foraging in lost drawers
          where once shiny cutlery
              made statements of a world
dying to be done with

repetitious understanding
                    will haunt you as day
          turn into goodbye
              an old man once said
when confronted with winds
                    that he had no objection
          being born as he was
              into this world's sweet misery
with one eye clapping

Bengt O Björklund – Days of Dark Thunder

crossing water melting ire
                        morning salutations
are early winds in early trees

sublet dreams in cities
                        stopped at roadblocks
tend to bleed

where battleships roll
                        waves will sing
seagull seaweed songs

men at war
                        wake up at dawn
preparing for battle

blind cruelty roar
                        in days
of distant thunder

a morning wind finds you
                        daring mortality
with your own blood

Bengt O Björklund – Days of Dark Thunder

the night was a pale mistress
                        whispering dark streets to life

            invitingly standing in doorways
                    turning cars into songs
                            coming from a jukebox

there is no place like here
                                where trams need no
                    tracks
            kites with wishbone tails
                    see birds feed their nestlings
                            in days to come

winners at the lottery melt
                                squalor into tin soldiers
                marching across the carpet
                        parental anguish is a ship
                            herding young islands

Bengt O Björklund – Days of Dark Thunder

Bengt O Björklund – Poet, Artist, Djembe player

Bengt O Björklund (born 1949 in Stockholm) is a Swedish poet, artist, and musician based in Västerhaninge, a few miles outside of Stockholm, Sweden. His life and work are closely intertwined — shaped by travel, resilience, and a lifelong search for a creative expression.
In 1968, at the age of 19, he was imprisoned in Turkey for a small amount of cannabis. During his five years there, he began to write and paint, turning a harsh experience into the starting point of an artistic and poetic journey. And the journey continues.
Björklund's poetry is influenced by the Beat Generation and by poets like Dylan Thomas, William Blake and Eastern forms such as haiku.
His collections — including I Missed Woodstock, I and If There is no Tomorrow. reflect themes of freedom, transformation, and everyday observation. But they are also often surrealistic and with a critical view of our present times.
In 2018, he was appointed Sweden Beat Poet Laureate for Life by the National Beat Poetry Foundation (USA).
Bengt has also had many art exhibitions. Most recently at the Nehru Centre in London. The band Beat Poet Society turns his poetry into music. Their album Ricochet of a Virus can be found on YouTube and Spotify.